Just us

The **BEST FRIENDS** Book

ABOUT US!

all about me

Lilly

Most of the time I am ...
thinking ✓
laughing ○
talking ○
dreaming ○

My home is ...
comfy ○
crowded ✓
clean ○
messy ○
huge ○

My room is ...
all mine ○
shared ✓
stylish ○
in need of a makeover ✓

I live ...
in a mansion ○
in an apartment ○
on a farm ○
somewhere else ✓

I do what I am told ...
all the time ○
most of the time ✓
hardly ever ○

My family is ...
big ✓
small ○
noisy ○
quiet ✓
unique ✓

The worst possible punishment is ...
no allowance ✓
no phone ○
no parties ○

My friends are ...
like family ✓
like me ✓
like-minded ✓

The best place to hang out with my friends is ...

at home ✓

at school ○

at clubs ○

The latest I have ever stayed up with my friends is ...

before 9 p.m. ○

after 9 p.m. ○

all night ✓

I read books ...

in bed ✓

on the bus ○

in the car ○

I love social media for ...

news ✓

friends ✓

celebrities ○

I don't love it ○

Some day I will ...

be rich ○

be famous ○

travel the world ✓

save the planet ✓

my
friends

Ask your friends and family to help you fill in this book. Get them to sign their names above the questions they answer.

This book was completed with help from:

signed
Lilly

Romantic movies make me ...

laugh ⦿
cry ◯
smile ◯

signed
Lilly

I am ...

busy ◯
cautious ⦿
adventurous ⦿

signed
Lilly

Most of the time, my hair is ...

a mess ⦿
stylish ◯
too long ◯

signed
Lilly

Under my bed, it's ...

neat and clean ◯
a disaster zone ⦿
I never look ⦿

signed
Sara Sara

When I'm embarrassed, I ...

blush ◉

laugh ◉

cry ◯

signed
Sara Sara

Some day I'd like to ...

see the world ◉

fly to the moon ◉

live in a castle ◉

signed
Lilly

The best things in life are ...

free ◉

worth working for ◯

expensive ◉

signed
Sara Sara

If I could, I would be ...

a dancer ◉

a doctor ◯

a dog trainer ◯

signed
Sara Sara

Writing a letter is ...

very thoughtful ◯

very boring ◉

very retro ◯

signed
Sara Sara

I have a big ...

mouth ◉

heart ◉

head ◉

This book was completed with help from:

Sara

When it's raining outside, I like to …

watch TV
read a book ●
message friends ○

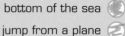
Sara

I will never …

dive to the bottom of the sea ●
jump from a plane
walk a tightrope ●

Sara

Circus clowns are …

scary ●
cute ○
funny

Sara

The best place for lunch is …

a restaurant ○
a park
a beach

Sara

My style is …

unique ●
on trend ○
always changing

Sara

The month I like best is …

April ○
July ○
October ○
December

signed

Lilly

The best place to see a movie is …

in a movie theater ○
at home ○
in the car ○

signed

Lilly

My family is …

funny ○
smart ○
sporty ○

signed

Lilly

Watching other people's vlogs is …

fascinating ○
a waste of time ○
great for getting ideas ○

signed

Lilly

I have this many brothers:

none ○
too many ○
enough ○

signed

Lilly

Surprises are …

exciting ○
embarrassing ○
better to give
than receive ○

signed

Lilly

My room is …

shared with my sibling ○
shared with my pet ○
all mine ○

face TO

all about your family

Sign your names, and then take turns completing the survey.

NAME *Sara*

Oldest person in your entire family

Dad

Most unusual name

Latney

Most unusual talent

Putting Swords Down

Best cook in your house

Zach

Funniest person

Leah? Mrs. Katie\ Mrs. J

Who do you look most like?

Hannah \ Beth

Most individual person

Grace

Would you prefer a bigger or smaller family?

Bigger

Where would you love to live?

Hawai'i or Bermuda

face

NAME *Lilly*

Oldest person in your entire family

Dad

Most unusual name

Larry

Most unusual talent

lick my elbow

Best cook in your house

Mom, Dad

Funniest person

Pop

Who do you look most like?

Mom   Dad

Most individual person

Me

Would you prefer a bigger or smaller family?

I like it

Where would you love to live?

in my Bed

could you be summer break besties

You're best friends at school and hang out together in your free time, but what if you went away together? Would two weeks strengthen the bond between you and your besties, or would 24/7 contact lead to catastrophe?

1. Write your names at the top of the grid.

2. Read the list, and then rate how important you think each feature is, from 0 (not at all important) to 5 (very important).

3. Decide which two friends to compare. Write their names at the top of the grid on the next page, and then, starting with question "a," subtract the lower score from the higher score and put the answer in the blue box.

4. Add up all the scores and enter the total in the pink box.

write names here

		Lily	Sara				
a	Sandy beaches	1	2				
b	Swimming pool	5	5				
c	Camping	5	5				
d	Shopping	3	5				
e	Hiking	9	5				
f	Time by yourself	100	100				
g	Flying in a plane	4	5				
h	Sports	5	5				
i	Theme parks	4	5				
j	Day trips	5	5				

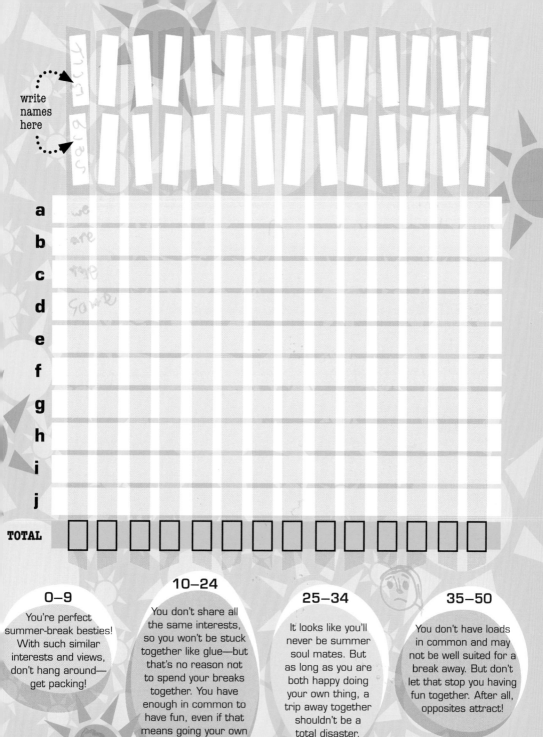

write
names
here

a
b
c
d
e
f
g
h
i
j

TOTAL

0–9

You're perfect summer-break besties! With such similar interests and views, don't hang around—get packing!

10–24

You don't share all the same interests, so you won't be stuck together like glue—but that's no reason not to spend your breaks together. You have enough in common to have fun, even if that means going your own way once in a while.

25–34

It looks like you'll never be summer soul mates. But as long as you are both happy doing your own thing, a trip away together shouldn't be a total disaster.

35–50

You don't have loads in common and may not be well suited for a break away. But don't let that stop you having fun together. After all, opposites attract!

the 5 best things about ...

name Lilly

1 She is weird

2 Needs lots of Help

3 friendly

4 amazing

5 herself

signed
Gavin Daniels

the **5** **best** things
about ...

name ~~Billy~~ Sara

1. Crazzy

2. Funny

3. needs help

4. needs more help

5. needs lot lot lots of HELP

signed Lilly

are you a
bestie
brainiac?

Do you know each other as well as you think?

Fabulous Food

	Names and	Names and
Best pizza topping		
Best ice cream		
Best chocolate treat		
Best breakfast		
Best vegetable		
	Score	Score

	Names and	Names and
Best cold drink		
Best cereal		
Best snack		
Best fruit		
Worst dessert		
	Score	Score

1) Choose a survey and write your names at the top of one of the columns.

2) Take turns guessing each other's answer, and then write down your score. If you both guess correctly, you score 2 points. If only one of you guesses correctly, you score just 1 point, and if neither of you guesses correctly, you score 0.

3) When you've finished the survey, add your scores together to give a total out of 10.

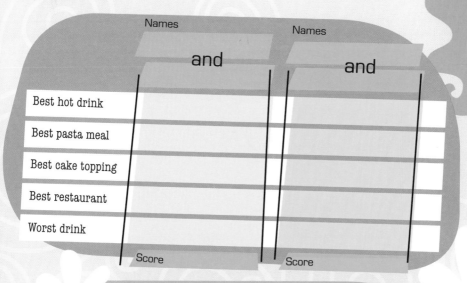

	Names and	Names and
Best hot drink		
Best pasta meal		
Best cake topping		
Best restaurant		
Worst drink		
	Score	Score

	Names and	Names and
Best toast topping		
Best milkshake		
Best cookie		
Best sweet treat		
Worst food ever		
	Score	Score

Check your scores

0–3 Maybe you haven't known each other long, or maybe you need to pay a little more attention to each other!

4–6 You're tuned into your pal's preferences, but there's always more to learn.

7–10 Wow! Are you twins?

who will be the first to go to Hollywood?

Are you on a fast track to fame?

Take a track each. Answer the questions and shade a square for each point you score. When you have answered all the questions, find the last star you passed over for your result.

start here

1

Have you ever entered a talent show?
Yes (2)
Yes and I won! (4)
No way! (0)

4

What's the best reward for doing a good performance?
Applause (5)
Praise (3)
Money (1)

You are destined to excel out of the limelight.

2

Do you practice your autograph?
All the time (3)
Occasionally (2)
Never (0)

3

How do you handle criticism?
I get upset (1)
I work hard to prove it wrong (2)
I take it to heart and try to improve (3)

5

Do you dress to ..
be comfortable? (0)
stand out? (3)
impress your friends? (2)

You have a foot on the fame ladder, but you need to work harder if you want to shine!

6

**o you love to
arn new skills?**

s, the more
e better (3)

ly if I'm
terested (2)

t really (0)

It looks like
you've got
what it takes
to be a star!

7

**Would you rather have
a stack of birthday cards
or a stack of fan mail?**

Birthday cards (1)

Fan mail (5)

8

**How would you feel
if your performance
received bad reviews?**

Angry (2)

Embarrassed (1)

Happy to have
some publicity (5)

10

**Do you believe
you have a
unique talent?**

Not really (0)

Maybe not unique,
but I'm definitely
talented (3)

Absolutely (5)

Fame may come
knocking on
your door, but
will you open it?

9

**If you were papped,
would you …**

cover your face? (0)

strike a pose? (3)

pretend to be
shocked but pose at
the same time? (4)

**With your
style and attitude,
you could be
a superstar!**

friend links

Make special connections between your **friends**! List their names here, and then write them in the grid on the right. Where possible, link the names like a **crossword puzzle**. When you finish, turn the grid into a **word search** by filling the blank boxes with random letters. Then challenge a friend to find all the names in less than a minute.

names

face TO

all about school

NAME _Sara_

Best class

Math

Worst class

_S.S._

Best teacher

Ms. Mckew

Coolest thing in my school

Most annoying thing about school

Funniest thing I ever saw at school

Person I have been friends with the longest

Best thing about lunch break

What I'm looking forward to most this year

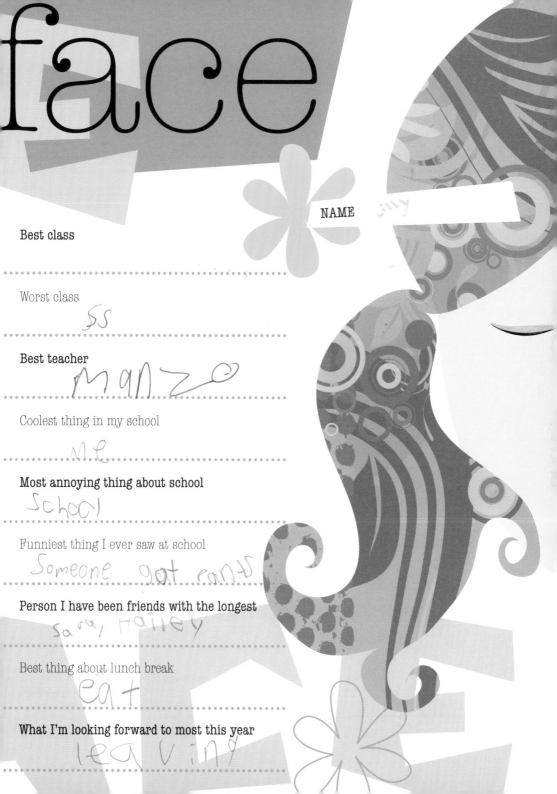

face

NAME Lilly

Best class

....

Worst class

SS

....

Best teacher

Manze

....

Coolest thing in my school

ME

....

Most annoying thing about school

School

....

Funniest thing I ever saw at school

Someone got pants

....

Person I have been friends with the longest

Sara, Hailey

....

Best thing about lunch break

eat

....

What I'm looking forward to most this year

leaving

....

friendship rings

name

name

What do you have in common with your circle of **friends**?

Write your friends' names in the flowers.

In the spaces where the rings cross over, write one thing the "owners" of the rings **have in common** with each other.

name

name

me

name

ends

the **5** best things

about ...

name ....

1

2

3

4

5

signed

the 5 best things about ...

name

1

2

3

4

5

signed

are you a
bestie
brainiac?

Do you know each other as well as you think?

Entertainment

	Names ___ and ___	Names ___ and ___
Best YouTube channel		
Top TV show		
Worst actor		
Best movie		
Top stage show		
	Score	Score

	Names ___ and ___	Names ___ and ___
Best vlogger		
Best group		
Best female singer		
Worst singer		
Best magazine		
	Score	Score

1) Choose a survey and write your names at the top of one of the columns.

2) Take turns guessing each other's answer, and then write down your score. If you both guess correctly, you score 2 points. If only one of you guesses correctly, you score just 1 point, and if neither of you guesses correctly, you score 0.

3) When you've finished the survey, add your scores together to give a total out of 10.

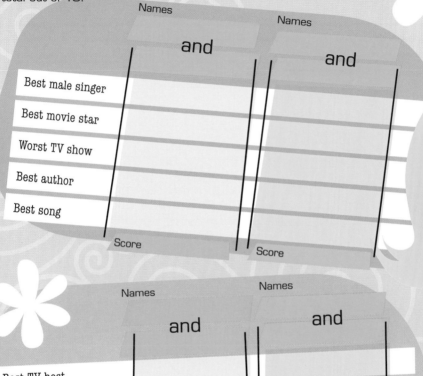

	Names and	Names and
Best male singer		
Best movie star		
Worst TV show		
Best author		
Best song		
	Score	Score

	Names and	Names and
Best TV host		
Best radio show		
Worst TV host		
Vinyl or download?		
Best TV talent show		
	Score	Score

Check your scores

0–3 You don't seem to know much about each other. You *are* friends, aren't you?

4–6 You're tuned in to your friend's tastes, but there's plenty of room to know each other better.

7–10 You know so much about each other— you must be siblings!

Life
choices

Life is full of possibilities.
What will you choose?

DRINKS

Soda
OR
Juice

HAIR

Short and neat
OR
Long and wavy

BIRTHDAYS

Presents
OR
Money

MORNINGS

Up early
OR
Sleep in

SEASONS

Summer
OR
Winter

SWIMMING POOL

Laps
OR
Raft

SPORTS

On the team
OR
Cheerleading

AT NIGHT

Read in bed
OR
Straight to sleep

SHOES

Flats
OR
Heels

EATING OUT

Pizza
OR
Burger

TRAVEL IN TIME

Past
OR
Future

MY ROOM

Personal space
OR
Party place

are you a bestie brainiac?

Do you know each other as well as you think?

Random Things

Strawberry or chocolate ice cream?	Names and		Names and	
Ketchup or mayonnaise?				
Bread or crackers?				
Rock or R&B?				
Carrots or peas?				
	Score		Score	

Cornflakes or toast?	Names and		Names and	
Ice-skating or dancing?				
Eggs or bacon?				
Green or purple?				
Gymnastics or football?				
	Score		Score	

1) Choose a survey and write your names at the top of one of the columns.

2) Take turns guessing each other's answer, and then write down your score. If you both guess correctly, you score 2 points. If only one of you guesses correctly, you score just 1 point, and if neither of you guesses correctly, you score 0.

3) When you've finished the survey, add your scores together to give a total out of 10.

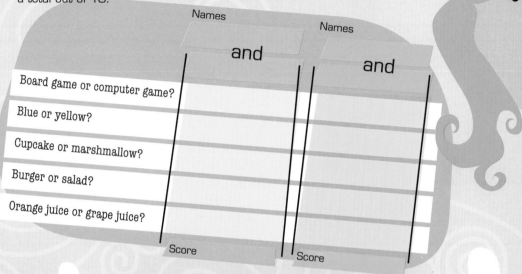

Names

and

Names

and

Board game or computer game?

Blue or yellow?

Cupcake or marshmallow?

Burger or salad?

Orange juice or grape juice?

Score

Score

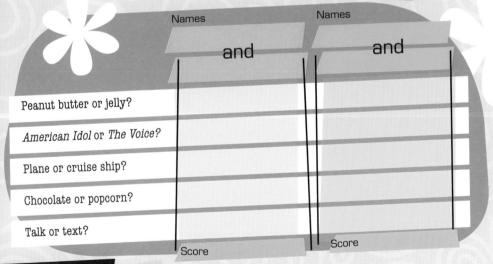

Names

and

Names

and

Peanut butter or jelly?

American Idol or The Voice?

Plane or cruise ship?

Chocolate or popcorn?

Talk or text?

Score

Score

Check your scores

 0–3 Uh-oh—either you just met or you need to spend some quality time together!

4–6 You know each other well but still have more to learn.

7–10 Great score! You're best buddies, right?

face TC

Extremes

Sign your names, and then take turns completing the survey.

NAME

Longest car trip

···

Longest time away from home

···

Latest bedtime

···

Earliest wake-up call

···

Greatest achievement

···

Best party

···

Longest phone call

···

Best present

···

Best exam result

···

face

NAME

Longest car trip

Longest time away from home

Latest bedtime

Earliest wake-up call

Greatest achievement

Best party

Longest phone call

Best present

Best exam result

family
links

Make a special connection between all the members of your **family**! List their names here, and then write them in the grid on the right. Where possible, link the names like a **crossword puzzle**. When you finish, turn the grid into a **word search** by filling the blank boxes with random letters. Then challenge a member of your family to find all the names in less than a minute.

names

....

....

....

....

....

....

....

family

the 5 best things about ...

name ....

1

2

3

4

5

signed

the **5** **best** things about ...

name ....

1

2

3

4

5

signed

who's the **biggest** risk-taker ?

Take a trip along the track to see how much you relish risk!

Take a track each. Answer the questions and shade a square for each point you score. When you have answered all the questions, go to the last green box you passed over for your risk reading!

start here

1
Do you ask people what they want before you buy them a gift?
Sometimes (2)
Never (5)
Always (1)

You like to play it safe and know what's around every corner. Why not let a few surprises into your life—it could be fun!

4
Have you ever radically changed your hairstyle?
Yes (4)
No (1)

2
You're buying a hat and you see one you like in the first store you enter. They have only one left in that style. Do you ...
buy it right away? (2)
keep looking and come back later if you don't find something else you like? (4)
ask the shop assistant to hold it for you, while you look around? (0)

3
Your friend is buying ice-cream cones and offers to buy you one. Do you ...
request a particular kind? (1)
say, "I'll have whatever you're having?" (3)
say, "Surprise me?" (4)

5
If you sent a valentine, would you ...
sign your name? (4)
sign a fake name? (1)
leave it blank? (0)

You are naturally cautious, but you're prepared to take a risk if the reward is worth it.

6

Would you let your best friend pick out your prom outfit?

Yes (4)

No (1)

Maybe (2)

You're a natural risk-taker, but you know when to reject risks for a more predictable path!

7

Pick one of the following jobs:

Dog walker (2)

Pet groomer (1)

Crocodile keeper (4)

Horse trainer (3)

8

Have you ever planned a surprise party for a friend?

Yes (3)

No (0)

10

You are at a fancy restaurant. The menu is in French and you don't understand a word! What do you do?

Pick a meal at random. (4)

Ask the waiter to explain the dishes. (2)

Stick to the bread basket. (0)

You can quickly assess a situation, and you know when to take a chance or run from risks— the perfect balance!

9

Would you appear on a reality TV show?

No way! (0)

Why not! (4)

Try and stop me! (5)

110% risk-taker! You have no fear and love the excitement of not knowing what will happen next!

face TO

Sign your names, and then take turns completing the survey.

The first movie you saw at a movie theater

··

The food you liked best when you were little

··

How you felt on your first day at school?

··

First play you performed in

··

Age of first bike ride without training wheels

··

First roller-coaster ride

··

First best friend

··

First pet

··

First prize you won

··

NAME

face

NAME

The first movie you saw at a movie theater

....

The food you liked best when you were little

....

How you felt on your first day at school?

....

First play you performed in

....

Age of first bike ride without training wheels

....

First roller-coaster ride

....

First best friend

....

First pet

....

First prize you won

....

are you a bestie brainiac?

Do you know each other as well as you think?

Dreams and Wishes

	Names ___ and ___	Names ___ and ___
Be rich or famous?		
Be a movie star or a rock star?		
Be an author or a songwriter?		
Be a dancer or a skater?		
Be a fashion designer or an artist?		
	Score	Score

	Names ___ and ___	Names ___ and ___
Learn to drive a car or learn to fly a plane?		
Be a vlogger or a DJ?		
Learn to paint or learn to draw?		
Learn French or learn Spanish?		
Design your own house or design your own clothes?		
	Score	Score

1) Choose a survey and write your names at the top of one of the columns.

2) Take turns guessing each other's answer, and then write down your score. If you both guess correctly, you score 2 points. If only one of you guesses correctly, you score just 1 point, and if neither of you guesses correctly, you score 0.

3) When you've finished the survey, add your scores together to give a total out of 10.

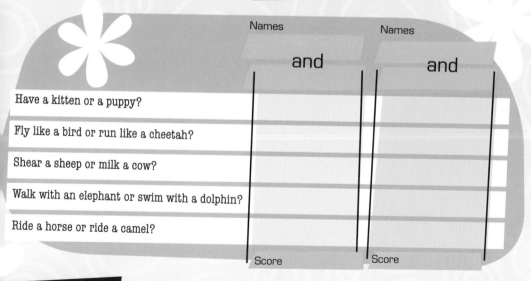

	Names and	Names and
Live in the country or live by the ocean?		
Live in a penthouse or live on a farm?		
Have a swimming pool or a tennis court?		
Have your own bathroom or a walk-in closet?		
Have a hot tub or a bowling alley?		
	Score	Score

	Names and	Names and
Have a kitten or a puppy?		
Fly like a bird or run like a cheetah?		
Shear a sheep or milk a cow?		
Walk with an elephant or swim with a dolphin?		
Ride a horse or ride a camel?		
	Score	Score

Check your scores

0–3 Spend some time talking about your dreams, and your friendship will grow and grow!

4–6 You know each other well—your bond can only get deeper!

7–10 You have a great connection and really understand your buddy's dreams and wishes!

fantasy Fortune cookies

1 Take the number of letters in your first name (this must be your full name, not a nickname). Then work out what number day of the week it is and add these two numbers together. So, if your name is Ashley and it is Tuesday, your number is: 6 + 3 = 9.

2 Starting in the nibbled segment of the "Talent" cookie, move clockwise around the circle, taking the same number of steps as your number. This will tell you what you will be famous for.

3 The "Talent" segment you land on will have a number. Move onto the "City" cookie and using that number, start at the nibbled segment and work your way around to see where you will live.

4 Continue in the same way to find out your future home!

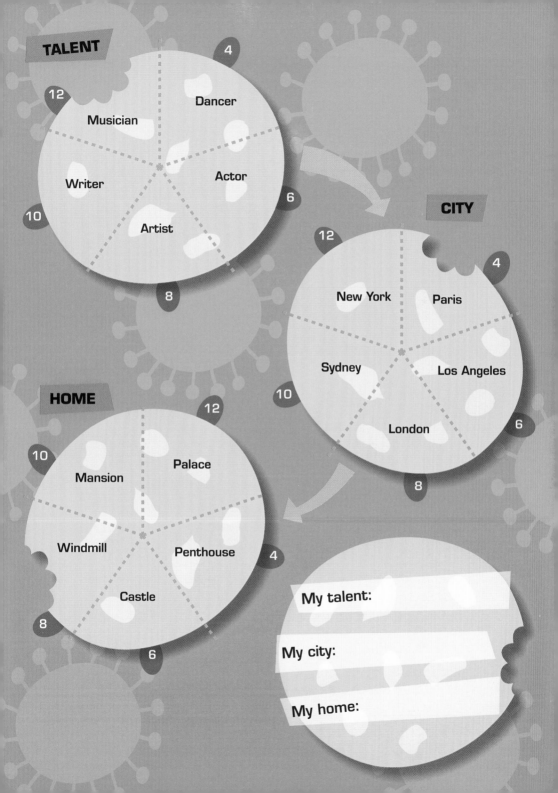

TALENT

Dancer
Musician
Actor
Writer
Artist

12
4
6
8
10

CITY

New York
Paris
Sydney
Los Angeles
London

12
4
6
8
10

HOME

Palace
Mansion
Windmill
Penthouse
Castle

12
4
6
8
10

My talent:

My city:

My home:

the 5 best things about ...

name ....

1

2

3

4

5

signed

the **5** **best** things about ...

name
....

1

2

3

4

5

signed

face TO

all about superhuman powers

What's the first thing you would do if ...

you were invisible?

you could hear through walls?

you could jump over buildings?

you could run faster than a train?

you could travel back in time?

you could travel to the future?

you could change the weather?

you could understand every language?

you could see in the dark?

NAME

face

NAME

you were invisible?

you could hear through walls?

you could jump over buildings?

you could run faster than a train?

you could travel back in time?

you could travel to the future?

you could change the weather?

you could understand every language?

you could see in the dark?

life
choices

Life is full of possibilities.
What will you choose?

SNACKS

Sweet
OR
Salty

JEANS

Black
OR
Blue

PARTIES

Sit and chat
OR
Sing and dance

RESTAURANTS

Fancy
OR
Casual

PETS

Cute and cuddly
OR
Big and boisterous

TRIPS AWAY

Relaxing
OR
Having an
adventure

TRAVEL BY

Plane
OR
Train

MAKING

Slime
OR
Scented soap

BREAKFAST

Toast
OR
Cereal

BED

Bouncy
OR
Firm

NIGHT OUT

Movie
OR
Show

KEEPING IN TOUCH

Call
OR
Text

TV

Comedy
OR
Drama

How would you

CONFLICTED

spooked

ecstatic

SHOCKED

ANGRY

happy

anxious

UPSET

unconcerned

CONFUSED

annoyed

EXCITED

nervous

confident

worried

sad

afraid

gloomy

BORED

SURPRISED

delighted

AMAZED

?

feel

- Your parents double your allowance.
- Your best friend doesn't reply to your messages.
- **You can't find your purse.**
- Your brother borrows your phone without asking.
- You receive two secret valentine cards.
- **It's the last day of the school break.**
- It's the first day of the new school year.
- Your best friend says she's changing her hair but won't say how.
- **It's the morning of your test results.**
- You're asked to sit next to the new girl in class and you haven't met her yet.
- You're on the last page of a fantastic book.
- **You have five minutes before the store closes, and you need to pick out a new pair of shoes.**
- It's the first night of the school play, and you're about to step onto the stage.
- Your family is moving to France.
- **You've been offered tickets to see the coolest band, but it will mean missing your friend's party.**
- You drop your phone and the screen cracks.
- You can only go to your friend's party if you clean your room first.
- **You made a shopping list but lost it, and now you have to try to remember everything you need to buy.**
- Your bus leaves in 20 minutes. You have your ticket, but it will take 15 minutes to get to the bus stop.

hero links

Make a list of all the people you **admire**—you don't have to know them personally and they don't even have to be alive! List their names here, and then write them in the grid on the right. Where possible, link the names like a **crossword puzzle**. When you finish, turn the grid into a **word search** by filling the blank boxes with random letters. Then challenge a friend to find all the names in less than a minute.

names

....
....
....
....
....
....
....
....

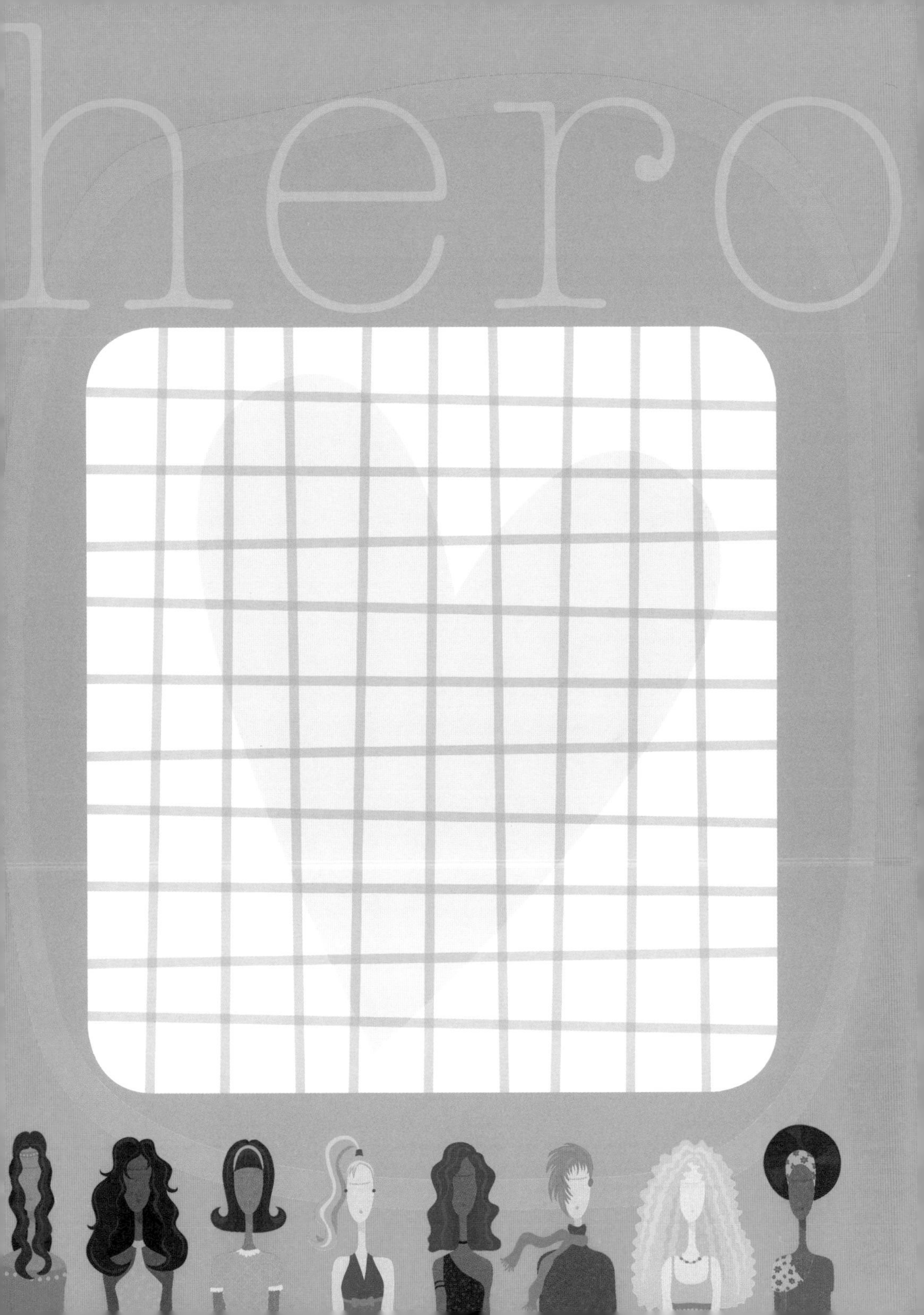
hero

family

friendship rings

name

name

What do you have in common with your **family**?

Write the names of five of your relatives in the flowers.

In the spaces where the rings cross over, write one thing the "owners" of the rings **have in common** with each other.

name

me

name

name

town OR country

CHECK YOUR %

BRAIN mix!

Start at the heart

% town   % country

Do you love the excitement and glamour of living in the city, or do you prefer the fresh air and freedom of life in the country?

Answer the questions and work your way around the wheel to discover your town or country brain mix. Excitement and glamour, or fresh air and freedom— it all adds up to 100% you!

1 If you had a choice, would you rather travel by …

taxi? **Move around 4**

bus? **Move around 2**

horseback? **Move around 0**

2 Which is best?

Ballet **Move around 2**

Barn dance **Move around 0**

Street dance **Move around 4**

3 Do you like to stay up late?

Yes, as often as I'm allowed to **Move around 4**

No, I'd rather get up early **Move around 0**

Sometimes **Move around 2**

4 If you had the choice, would you rather live in …

a windmill? **Move around 0**

a penthouse? **Move around 4**

a houseboat? **Move around 2**

5 Which of these activities do you enjoy the most?

Swimming **Move around 2**

Shopping **Move around 4**

Hiking **Move around 0**

face TO

desert-island dreams

If you lived on a desert island and could only have one of each of the following things, what would you choose?

Something for communicating with the outside world

Luxury item—money is no object!

NAME

Item from your bedroom

Item from your bathroom cupboard

Electronic item

Creative hobby

Game

Book

Item of footwear

face

NAME

Something for communicating with the outside world

....

Luxury item—money is no object!

....

Item from your bedroom

....

Item from your bathroom cupboard

....

Electronic item

....

Creative hobby

....

Game

....

Book

....

Item of footwear

....

if you were a millionaire

Write your friends' names at the top of the wish lists, and then write two things you would give them if money were no object and one thing you could give them that money cannot buy.

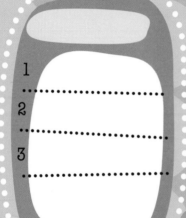

1 ....

2 ....

3 ....

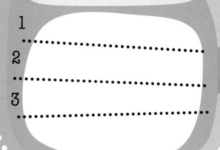

1 ....

2 ....

3 ....

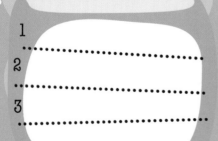

1 ....

2 ....

3 ....

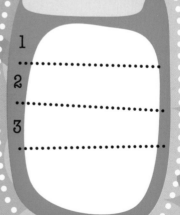

1 ....

2 ....

3 ....

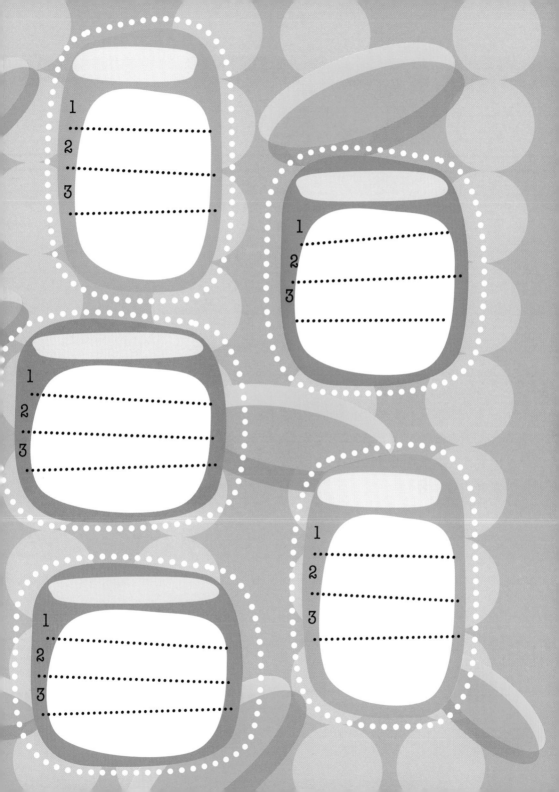

what's your SFQ?

Everyone has something special to bring to a friendship: their SFQ, or "Special Friendship Quality." Pick five words that best describe you, and then find out your SFQ.

energetic

loving

funny

careful

gentle

smart

quiet

outrageous

creative

confident

sporty

opinionated

thoughtful

focused

loud

shy

cautious

brave

could you be roommates

You might think you've got a lot in common, but what if you were roomies? Could you share a space with grace, or would bad chemistry create a room of doom?

1. Write your names in the white boxes at the top of the grid.

2. Read the list below, and then rate how important you think each feature is in a dream room, from 0 (not at all important) to 5 (very important).

3. Decide which two friends to compare. Write their names at the top of the grid on the next page, and then, starting with question "a," subtract the lower score from the higher score and put the answer in the pink box.

4. Add up the scores and enter the total in the green box.

write names here ...▶

a	Bright walls					
b	Super tidy					
c	Room for pets					
d	Posters on the wall					
e	Own bathroom					
f	Lots of bookshelves					
g	Spare beds for sleepovers					
h	Special snack drawer					
i	Extra-large closets					
j	Wall space for a 72-inch TV					

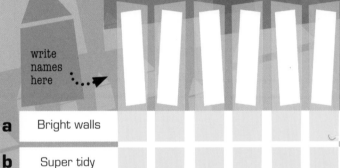

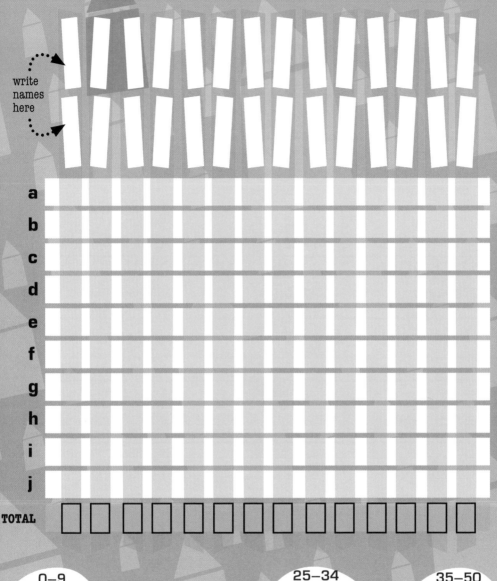

write names here

a
b
c
d
e
f
g
h
i
j

TOTAL

0–9

You make perfect roomies. With your similar styles, you'll get along like a house on fire!

10–24

You're not a perfect match, but as long as you are aware of each other's personal space, you should make respectable roommates.

25–34

You might be best friends, but your roomie rating suggests you might not get on in close quarters for more than a few days!

35–50

Besties beware! Your rating suggests that if you dare to share, sparks are going to fly, so maybe you should stick to sleepovers!

are you a
bestie
brainiac?

Do you know each other as well as you think?

Have you ever …

	Names ___ and ___		Names ___ and ___	
lived in another country?				
been in a limousine?				
swam in the sea?				
visited a TV studio?				
made your own earrings?				
	Score		Score	

	Names ___ and ___		Names ___ and ___	
lost your phone?				
written a novel?				
entered a singing competition?				
come first in a sports event?				
cut your own hair?				
	Score		Score	

1) Choose a survey and write your names at the top of one of the columns.
2) Take turns guessing each other's answer, and then write down your score. If you both guess correctly, you score 2 points. If only one of you guesses correctly, you score just 1 point, and if neither of you guesses correctly, you score 0.
3) When you've finished the survey, add your scores together to give a total out of 10.

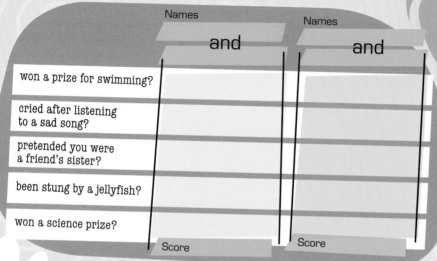

Names **and**   Names **and**

won a prize for swimming?

cried after listening to a sad song?

pretended you were a friend's sister?

been stung by a jellyfish?

won a science prize?

Score   Score

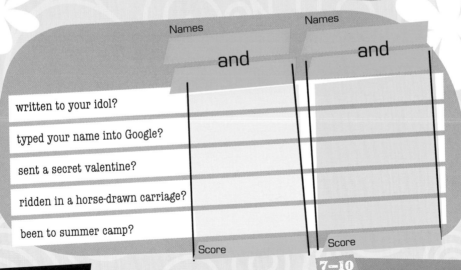

Names **and**   Names **and**

written to your idol?

typed your name into Google?

sent a secret valentine?

ridden in a horse-drawn carriage?

been to summer camp?

Score   Score

Check your scores

0–3 Have a sleepover and get to know each other better!

4–6 You have more to learn about each other, but your score says you are friends who care.

7–10 True BFFs! Your high score shows that you love to listen as well as talk and are genuinely interested in each other's experiences.

face TO

all about the future **in 20 years' time**

Sign your names, and then take turns completing the survey.

NAME

I'll be living in (which country?)

....

City / Countryside / By the ocean?

....

Penthouse / House / Mansion / Windmill / Other?

....

Will I be married?

....

Children? How many?

....

Career

....

I'll be famous for ...

....

I will have won these awards ...

....

I will have visited ...

....

face

NAME

I'll be living in (which country?)

....

City / Countryside / By the ocean?

....

Penthouse / House / Mansion / Windmill / Other?

....

Will I be married?

....

Children? How many?

....

Career

....

I'll be famous for ...

....

I will have won these awards ...

....

I will have visited ...

....

most likely to ...

Think of your friends and family,
and then decide who is most likely to ...

write a best-selling book?

....

sail around the world?

....

become a world leader?

....

become a movie star?

....

invent names for their children?

....

live on a farm?

....

design their own home?

....

snorkel the Great Barrier Reef?

....

be a sports star?

....

be a rock star? ....

have their own TV show? ....

work in a foreign country? ....

design their own clothes? ....

become a scientist? ....

fly to the moon? ....

invent a new slime? ....

perform in a circus? ....

audition for a TV talent show? ....

become a vet? ....

become a doctor? ....